HOW NIGERIAN YOUTHS CAN AVOID VIOLENT EXTREMISM

AVOIDING VIOLENT EXTREMISM IN NIGERIA

ONUCHE E. SAMSON

ISBN: 9798870434414

DEDICATION

This book is dedicated to my Wife, Mrs Dorcas Onuche and My Daughter, the "DUE", My Parents, Mr Emmanuel Onuche Odugbo and Mrs Rosemary Onuche Odugbo, my Siblings and to all potential readers.

CONTENTS

CHAPTER ONE

INTRODUCTION

Understanding Violent Extremism

In the complex and ever-evolving landscape of Nigeria, one of the most pressing challenges faced by its youth is the allure of violent extremism. The allure of extremist ideologies, whether they are rooted in political, religious, or socioeconomic grievances, poses a real and immediate threat to the stability and unity of our great nation. The consequences of radicalization and violent extremism are devastating, both for those directly affected and for society as a whole.

In this section, we delve into the heart of the matter by unraveling the intricate web of violent extremism. We aim to shed light on its origins, its driving forces, and the factors that contribute to its persistence. Understanding this phenomenon is the first step toward countering it effectively and empowering the youth of Nigeria to avoid its dangerous path.

In Chapter 1, we embark on a historical journey, tracing the roots of violent extremism in Nigeria. By examining the historical context, we gain valuable insights into the deep-seated issues that continue to fuel extremist movements. We explore how political developments, economic disparities, and social tensions have all played a role in shaping the current landscape of extremism.

Chapter 2 delves into the core of the matter, focusing on the root causes of violent extremism. We explore the multifaceted nature of this issue, understanding that it is not born out of a single factor but a combination of various elements. We examine the role of socioeconomic disparities, political influences, and ideological motivations in driving individuals towards extremist ideologies. By comprehending these root causes, we can develop more effective strategies to address and prevent them.

Chapter 3 shifts our focus to recognizing the signs of radicalization. To effectively counter extremism, it's crucial to understand the behavioral indicators that may signal an individual's descent into extremism. This chapter also explores the role of online recruitment and radicalization, a growing concern in the digital age. We delve into the online platforms and tactics used by extremist groups to target vulnerable individuals and explore ways to combat online radicalization.

As we journey through this section, we encourage readers to keep in mind that the fight against violent extremism is not solely the responsibility of the government or security forces. It is a collective effort that involves families, communities, educators, and every Nigerian youth. By understanding the complexities of violent extremism, we empower ourselves with the knowledge needed to address this issue effectively and work toward a brighter, more secure future for our country.

In the following chapters, we will explore practical strategies and approaches to prevent the spread of extremist ideologies and promote resilience among Nigerian youths. We will also showcase inspiring success stories and examples of communities that have successfully countered extremism, offering hope and guidance to those who seek a path away from violence.

Let us begin this important journey toward understanding and ultimately countering violent extremism in Nigeria, as we work together to build a safer and more prosperous future for all. To this end, I will like to share personal experience and the reason this book is put together as follows:

PERSONAL EXPERIENCE AND CASE STUDIES

I have never seen someone so upset; Yakubu's face was in flames. Deep wrinkles spread gloriously across his face and he aged in that instant. I asked why he wasn't as cheerful as he used to be whenever he delivered water to the Corper's Lodge in Mani Area, Kastina State, Nigeria. I wondered how possible it was for someone to crease his face into a crooked scowl. Yakubu blurted out the reason for his anger in a poorly constructed Sentence, slurred by an Hausa accent. As terrible as his grammar was; I deduced he found the budding relationship between a male and female Corper (Corps Members) repulsive. His obvious disdain lay in the fact that they shared an apartment. Cohabitation was an alien ideology to him and that fascinated me. I brushed his tense shoulders slightly and went into my apartment; a mistake I still regret.

One evening, the sun had burned harshly during the day and we were glad for the fresh breeze that filtered in through the Window. We all left the Windows opened to usher in the auspicious presence of the late September wind. Everything was perfect until a shrill cry of a woman rang in the air, slicing through the silence that had settled on the Lodge. Instinctively, I darted to the door, dragging along an object for defense. Other Corpers (NYSC Members) in the Lodge were up too, all woken by the uproar. We dashed to the room where the sound had come from. Sprawled on the floor were the lovebirds that were cohabiting; wriggling in excruciating pain. I stared aghast at the horrid sight before me, alarm etched across my face. Blood gushed from their hands and painted the floor deep crimson.

"Yakubu and some Hausa boys" the lady half explained amidst tears. There was no time to further question them; they were rushed to the NYSC Secretariat for treatment. Later, we were told that Yakubu had brought his fellow Muslims who considered Cohabitation an unpardonable sin, to melt justice on the "sinners" by chopping off their fingers.

This incident in 2017, spurred me into committing time and resources into a movement organized by YALI (Young African Leaders Initiative) in collaboration with Action aid to educate many young people like Yakubu, who have misguided religious, cultural and political ideologies. This was something I should have done the day Yakubu had flared up. The YALI Network Members (Lokoja Chapter) burdened by this tale; have enlightened and sensitized communities on the need for Youths to channel their energy into Nation building rather than acts of violence. One of the most recent sanitization was at Ejule in Ofu Local Government Area of Kogi State. The one-day event emphasized the need to shun "Violent Extremism"; the message had a resounding effect coming from the mouth of the **Onu (King) of Ejule, ALHAJI ABDULLAHI A. AMANABA.**

It was necessary to take this timely message to Ejule because it is an area prone to violence. As a locality populated by Youths with ideologies as diverse as they are conflicting; Ejule has recorded disputes that have escalated into communal conflicts with casualties in recent past. Ejule as noted above, have been one of the most violent prone areas in the Eastern part of Kogi State, Nigeria, where a lot of Youths have been used by Politicians to perpetrate violence and disruption of peace. Hence, the need for our visit to sensitize the Youths against being used as objects in the hands of the politicians and to avoid any act capable of plunging them into becoming Violence Extremist, as recorded in the past. As a member of YALI Network, Kogi, in a speech delivered by me, I encouraged them to be "useful Youths" by engaging in productive and sustainable ventures that can stand the test of time, such as (1) forming a youth association that can take part in football competitions, (2) Cultural Display Group; where they can showcase their rich cultural heritage and it can be their passport to the World, (3) as these come together, our own part as YALIANS, will be to come from time to time to teach them entrepreneurial skills that can empower them for the future. Now, from the above 1-3, are the various steps which, when properly harnessed would emancipate the Youths not just in Ejule alone, but in our Rural Areas from being used as agents of violence, which over time had been their source of livelihood, there is a saying that *"an idle mind is the devil's workshop"* I couldn't agree more. A lot of them don't know what they can do to better their society as such they take on one of the "easiest but dangerous" venture, which is thuggery, impregnating underage girls and giving birth to children they cannot even cater for, the children who would recycle their fathers' life style. On our part, we try to discourage them and expose them to the better part of life to make them responsible citizens of the society. With my experience in the North on how a lot of Youths have been so confined to one a way life style, to the point that they cannot think on their own to do what is right as a result you see them so bitter when eventually they see any lifestyle contradicting what they have been taught and grown to believe, hence they resort to violence as a means of showing their grievance. The reason for my being part of an advocacy group such as "Young African Leaders Initiative", *"ActionAid"*, *"Kogi Earnest Group"* and the most recent, which was held in Abuja, at the International Conference Center, "Youth Decide" which is pioneered by the convener and co-convener, *"NOT TOO YOUNG TO RUN"* Bill, Samson Itodo and Hamzat Lawal as well as other notable young Nigerians like Chukwuma Ephraim Okenwa (C.E.O), and Ovo Otarigho is to make Nigerian Youths see the future that lie ahead of them and to shun any act capable of destroying the future.

CHAPTER TWO

The Landscape and Historical Context of Violent Extremism in Nigeria

Violent extremism has become an unsettling reality in Nigeria, a country known for its cultural diversity, natural beauty, and economic potential. The nation's landscape, both literal and figurative, has been profoundly shaped by the presence of extremist movements that threaten the stability and unity of the country.

Historical Context

To understand the current landscape of violent extremism in Nigeria, one must delve into the complex historical factors that have contributed to its emergence and persistence. Nigeria's history is marked by a series of events and circumstances that have provided fertile ground for the growth of extremist ideologies.

Colonial Legacy: The colonial history of Nigeria plays a crucial role in shaping the country's modern landscape of extremism. Nigeria was a British colony until it gained independence in 1960. During the colonial period, the British colonial administration divided Nigeria into distinct regions and imposed their administrative systems, often without regard for the existing ethnic, religious, and cultural boundaries. This arbitrary division created a fragmented nation with diverse ethnic and religious groups. The legacy of these divisions and the competition for limited resources have fueled identity-based tensions and grievances, which extremist groups have exploited.

Religious Diversity: Nigeria is known for its religious diversity, with a significant Muslim population in the north and a predominantly Christian population in the south. While this diversity has enriched the cultural tapestry of the nation, it has also been a source of tension. Extremist groups, like Boko Haram, have exploited religious differences, using religious narratives to justify their actions and recruit followers. The religious divide, combined with socioeconomic disparities, has made certain areas of Nigeria more susceptible to radicalization.

Post-Independence Political Turbulence: Nigeria's journey post-independence has been marked by a series of political upheavals, including military coups, decades of military rule, and contested elections. This political instability has created a sense of disenfranchisement and disillusionment among segments of the population. Extremist ideologies, in some cases, offer an alternative to the perceived failures of the political system.

Economic Disparities: Widespread poverty, income inequality, and economic disparities have been persistent challenges in Nigeria. These disparities have led to economic grievances among marginalized communities. Some individuals, especially youth facing limited economic opportunities, may be drawn to extremist groups that promise economic relief, justice, or a more equitable society.

Identity and Ethnic Conflicts: Nigeria's diverse ethnic groups and cultures have at times clashed over resources, power, and political representation. Ethnoreligious conflicts, often rooted in these identity-based tensions, have resulted in violence and displacement. Some extremist groups exploit these divisions and use them to justify their actions.

Regional Disparities: Economic and infrastructural disparities between Nigeria's regions have been a source of discontent. Northern regions, in particular, have faced underdevelopment, contributing to grievances that extremist groups exploit. Boko Haram, for example, has capitalized on the marginalization of certain communities in the north.

Understanding the historical context is essential to comprehend the multifaceted nature of violent extremism in Nigeria. This history has created a complex web of grievances, divisions, and vulnerabilities that extremist groups exploit. To address the issue effectively, one must consider these historical factors and their ongoing impact on the country's security and stability. In the following chapters, we will explore the root causes of violent extremism in greater detail, examining the socio-economic, political, and ideological influences that drive individuals towards extremist ideologies.

Current Challenges

The contemporary landscape of violent extremism in Nigeria is marked by a series of complex and interrelated challenges. These challenges have profound implications for the security, stability, and unity of the nation. Understanding these current issues is crucial for addressing the problem effectively.

Boko Haram: One of the most prominent extremist groups in Nigeria is Boko Haram. Founded in the early 2000s, this jihadist group, whose name loosely translates to "Western education is forbidden," has been responsible for a wave of violence and terror. Boko Haram is known for its ruthless tactics, including abductions, suicide bombings, and attacks on both civilians and security forces. The group's ideology is rooted in a radical interpretation of Islam, and it seeks to establish an Islamic state in northeastern Nigeria. The persistent threat posed by Boko Haram continues to destabilize the affected regions.Fulani Herdsmen Conflict: The conflict between nomadic Fulani herdsmen and settled farming communities, often in central and northern Nigeria, has escalated into violence in recent years. Disputes over land, resources, and grazing routes have fueled clashes, leading to loss of lives and property. While not all Fulani herdsmen are involved in violence, the actions of some groups have created tensions and added to the overall security challenges faced by the nation.

Separatist Movements: In the southeast, there are separatist movements like the Indigenous People of Biafra (IPOB) that advocate for the secession of the region from Nigeria. These movements challenge the unity of the country and have led to protests and confrontations with security forces.

Ethnoreligious Clashes: Ethnoreligious clashes between Christian and Muslim communities have periodically erupted in central Nigeria. These conflicts often involve disputes over land, resources, and political power. The clashes have resulted in tragic loss of life and the displacement of communities.

Economic Desperation: Widespread poverty, unemployment, and economic disparities persist in Nigeria. These economic factors make some individuals vulnerable to extremist narratives that promise a more just and equitable society. For some, joining extremist groups may seem like a way to escape economic hardship or find a sense of purpose.

Distrust in Government: A significant challenge lies in the population's lack of trust in the government's ability to address these security and socioeconomic challenges. The perception of government corruption, inefficiency, and failure to protect its citizens has led some communities to take matters into their own hands, contributing to a cycle of violence.

Regional Instability: Nigeria's security challenges are not isolated but are influenced by the broader regional context. Conflicts and extremist groups in neighboring countries, such as Mali and Niger, spill over into Nigeria, complicating efforts to maintain security and stability.

Addressing these current challenges is essential to combat violent extremism effectively in Nigeria. It requires a multifaceted approach that addresses the root causes of extremism, strengthens community resilience, and fosters trust in government institutions. By understanding the complexity of these challenges, policymakers, community leaders, and individuals can work together to find sustainable solutions that promote peace, security, and unity in Nigeria.

To truly understand the current landscape of violent extremism in Nigeria, one must delve into the historical roots of the issue. While violent extremism did not emerge overnight, historical events have contributed to its growth and persistence. Thus, we shall consider them in bits according to the subheads below.

Colonial Legacy: Nigeria's colonial history, marked by the division of various ethnic and religious groups, created a fractured society. These divisions sowed the seeds of identity-based tensions and grievances that continue to be exploited by extremist groups.

The colonial legacy of violent extremism refers to the enduring impact of colonial rule on societies and the potential role it plays in fostering conditions conducive to extremism and violence. It is important to note that this is a complex and nuanced topic, with various historical, social, economic, and political factors contributing to the development of violent extremism. Here are some aspects to consider:

Imposition of Borders: Colonial powers often drew arbitrary borders without regard for existing ethnic, tribal, or cultural divisions. This has led to the creation of artificial states that encompass diverse groups, sometimes resulting in internal conflicts and power struggles.

Divide and Rule Policies: Colonial powers frequently employed "divide and rule" strategies, exploiting existing ethnic, religious, or tribal tensions to maintain control. These divisions can persist long after independence, contributing to ongoing conflict and extremism.

Economic Exploitation: Colonization often involved the exploitation of natural resources and economic systems, leaving local populations impoverished. Economic disparities and lack of opportunities can contribute to frustration and radicalization.

Cultural Suppression: The suppression of indigenous cultures and imposition of foreign norms and values during colonial rule can create a sense of cultural alienation and identity crisis. Extremist groups may exploit this by offering a distorted sense of identity and purpose.

Legacy of Authoritarianism: Many former colonies inherited authoritarian structures from their colonial past. These structures may have contributed to political instability and a lack of inclusive governance, creating conditions ripe for extremism.

Weapon Proliferation: Colonial powers often left behind a legacy of militarization, providing arms and training to local groups. This militarization can contribute to a culture of violence and make it easier for extremist groups to access weapons.

Religious and Ethno-Nationalist Tensions: Colonial policies sometimes exacerbated religious or ethnic tensions. For example, the favoring of one group over another could create grievances that persist and contribute to extremism.

Educational Impact: The colonial education system often reinforced colonial narratives and values. This might result in a population with limited access to diverse perspectives and a susceptibility to extremist ideologies.

Resentment and Historical Grievances: Past injustices and violence perpetrated by colonial powers may create a sense of historical grievance, which can be exploited by extremist groups to garner support.

It is important to recognize that while the colonial legacy can contribute to the conditions conducive to violent extremism, it is not the sole determinant. Contemporary factors, such as geopolitics, governance, and global economic conditions, also play crucial roles in shaping the landscape of extremism in post-colonial societies.

Political Turbulence: Nigeria has experienced a series of political upheavals, including coups, military rule, and contested elections. Political instability has created fertile ground for extremist ideologies to take root.

Economic Disparities: Widespread poverty and economic inequalities have fueled discontent among the population, making some individuals vulnerable to extremist narratives that promise a more just and equitable society.

Religious and Ethnoreligious Factors: Nigeria's religious diversity has been a double-edged sword. While it has enriched the cultural tapestry of the nation, it has also been a source of tension, exploited by extremist groups to justify their actions and recruit followers.

Also, to better understand this phenomenon, I have to bring in so many factors, as follows

The contemporary landscape of violent extremism in Nigeria is marked by several significant challenges:

Boko Haram: The emergence of Boko Haram in the early 2000s marked a turning point in Nigeria's battle against extremism. This jihadist group, whose name loosely translates to "Western education is forbidden," has been responsible for countless acts of violence, including abductions, suicide bombings, and attacks on civilians and security forces.

Fulani Herdsmen Conflict: The conflict between nomadic Fulani herdsmen and settled farming communities has escalated into violence in some regions, further straining the country's social fabric.

Separatist Movements: In the southeast, groups like the Indigenous People of Biafra (IPOB) have agitated for secession, posing a challenge to the country's unity.

Ethno-religious Clashes: Ethno-religious clashes between Christian and Muslim communities have periodically erupted in central Nigeria, resulting in tragic loss of life.

Economic Desperation: Economic factors continue to drive some individuals toward extremist groups as they seek livelihood opportunities and a sense of belonging.

Distrust in Government: A lack of trust in the government's ability to address these challenges has led some communities to take matters into their own hands, contributing to a cycle of violence.

The landscape of violent extremism in Nigeria is complex, multifaceted, and constantly evolving. It is influenced by a combination of historical, political, socioeconomic, and religious factors. To effectively address this issue, it is essential to recognize and understand its various dimensions, as we'll further explore in the subsequent chapters of this book.

In the following chapters, we will delve deeper into the root causes of violent extremism in Nigeria, recognizing the signs of radicalization, and strategies to counter this pervasive issue. Together, we will seek solutions and approaches to empower Nigerian youths to avoid the path of extremism and contribute to a more peaceful and prosperous future for the nation.

CHAPTER THREE

The Root Causes of Violent Extremism

Socioeconomic Disparities: Economic grievances are among the most significant factors contributing to violent extremism in Nigeria. High levels of poverty, unemployment, and income inequality create a fertile ground for extremist recruitment. Many vulnerable individuals are lured into extremist groups with promises of economic relief, a sense of belonging, and opportunities for a better life. Extremist organizations often provide financial incentives, which can be especially appealing in areas where economic opportunities are scarce.

Political Marginalization: The perception of political marginalization, particularly in regions with ethnic or religious minorities, can lead to disenfranchisement and grievances. When communities feel excluded from political decision-making and representation, some individuals may turn to extremist ideologies as a means of expressing their discontent and seeking political change.

Religious and Ethnoreligious Factors: Nigeria's religious diversity, with a predominantly Muslim north and a largely Christian south, has at times been a source of tension and division. Extremist groups like Boko Haram exploit religious differences, using religious narratives to justify their actions and recruit followers. Ethnoreligious clashes, often rooted in identity-based tensions, further contribute to the cycle of violence.

Lack of Access to Education: Limited access to quality education, particularly in conflict-affected areas, hinders social and economic mobility. Extremist groups often target areas with low educational

23

infrastructure, using this vulnerability to their advantage. They may offer education that aligns with their ideologies, which can indoctrinate vulnerable youths.

Social Alienation: Some individuals, particularly young people, may experience social alienation, a sense of not belonging to the broader society. Extremist groups provide a sense of identity, purpose, and belonging to those who feel marginalized or isolated. This sense of belonging can be a powerful recruiting tool.

Revenge and Retribution: Personal or communal grievances, including grievances related to past violence, can motivate individuals to seek revenge and retribution through extremism. When communities have experienced violence or injustices, some may turn to extremist groups to address these wrongs.

Radicalization in Prisons: Prisons can serve as breeding grounds for extremist ideologies. Inmates may be exposed to radical beliefs and further radicalized during their incarceration. Upon release, they can become active members of extremist groups.

External Influences: The presence of external extremist groups, including transnational organizations, can exacerbate the situation in Nigeria. These groups often provide funding, training, and ideological support to local affiliates. They take advantage of existing grievances and instability to expand their influence.

Arms Proliferation: The widespread availability of small arms and light weapons in Nigeria exacerbates the impact of extremist violence. Easy access to weapons enables extremist groups to carry out attacks and defend their positions more effectively.

Weak Governance and Corruption: Corruption and weak governance undermine public trust in government institutions.

When communities perceive government officials as corrupt and ineffective, they may be less inclined to cooperate with authorities in the fight against extremism. This distrust can create opportunities for extremist groups to operate with relative impunity.

Understanding these root causes is crucial for developing effective strategies to counter violent extremism. It requires a comprehensive approach that addresses both the immediate security challenges and the underlying issues, such as poverty, education, and governance. By tackling these root causes, Nigerian authorities, civil society, and international partners can work to prevent the radicalization and recruitment of individuals into extremist groups.

CHAPTER FOUR

Recognizing the Signs of Radicalization

Recognizing the signs of radicalization is crucial for preventing the radicalization of individuals who may be susceptible to extremist ideologies or violence. Radicalization can occur in various contexts, including religious, political, or social movements. While it's essential to approach this topic with sensitivity and avoid making assumptions about people based on their beliefs or backgrounds, there are common signs and behaviors that may indicate radicalization. These signs can help friends, family members, educators, and authorities identify individuals who may be at risk. It's important to remember that the presence of one or more of these signs does not necessarily mean that someone is on a path to extremism, but they may warrant further investigation or intervention.

Some common signs of radicalization that we may think are socialization:

Sudden and Intense Ideological Shift: A noticeable shift in a person's beliefs or values, especially toward more extreme or radical ideologies, can be an early sign.

Isolation: Radicalized individuals often become increasingly isolated from friends and family who do not share their new beliefs. They may also avoid social activities and become withdrawn.

Online Activity: Extremist propaganda and recruitment efforts often take place online. Frequenting extremist websites, engaging with extremist content on social media, or expressing radical views online can be indicators.

Change in Appearance or Dress: A person might adopt a more extreme or militant appearance, such as wearing clothing associated with extremist groups.

Increased Hostility: Radicalized individuals may become more aggressive and hostile towards those who do not share their beliefs. They may advocate violence as a solution to their perceived grievances.

Loss of Interest in Previous Activities: A person's interests and hobbies may change drastically, as they become consumed by extremist ideologies and activities.

Sudden Changes in Relationships: Breaking ties with friends or family members who do not support their radical beliefs or forming new relationships with like-minded individuals can be a sign.

Travelling to Conflict Zones: Some individuals may travel to conflict zones or areas of terrorist activity to join extremist groups.

Secretive Behavior: Radicalized individuals may become secretive about their activities, contacts, or plans, making it difficult for friends and family to know what they are doing.

Expressions of Grievance: Frequent expressions of anger or grievances related to political, religious, or social issues can be an indication of radicalization.

Recruitment Attempts: Attempts to recruit others into extremist ideologies or groups, either in person or online, can be a clear sign of radicalization.

If you suspect someone is becoming radicalized, it's important to take a cautious and non-confrontational approach. You can seek help from mental health professionals, community organizations, or law enforcement, depending on the situation and the level of concern. The goal is to prevent violent extremism while respecting the individual's rights and privacy.

Efforts to counter radicalization should also include community-based programs and educational initiatives that promote tolerance, critical thinking, and open dialogue to address the underlying issues that make individuals susceptible to extremist ideologies.

CHAPTER FIVE

Understanding the role of Education and Awareness in curbing Extremism in Nigeria

Education and awareness on violent extremism are essential components of counterterrorism efforts aimed at preventing individuals from becoming radicalized and engaging in acts of violence. These initiatives focus on understanding the root causes of extremism, raising public awareness, and developing strategies to counteract the radicalization process. Here is a detailed account of education and awareness efforts on violent extremism:

Understanding Violent Extremism:

Education begins with a comprehensive understanding of the factors that drive individuals toward violent extremism. This includes studying the ideological, social, economic, and psychological factors that contribute to radicalization.

Public Awareness Campaigns:

Government agencies, non-governmental organizations (NGOs), and community groups often launch public awareness campaigns to inform the public about the dangers of violent extremism.

These campaigns aim to educate individuals about the signs of radicalization, how to report suspicious activities, and the importance of community resilience.

School-Based Programs:

Schools play a critical role in educating young people about the risks of extremism. Educational programs focus on critical thinking, tolerance, and understanding different perspectives to counteract extremist ideologies.These programs promote inclusive and diverse environments where students are less susceptible to radicalization.

Online Education:

Given the significant role of the internet in radicalization, online education programs provide information and resources to counter extremist narratives.

Organizations and governments create websites, social media campaigns, and interactive materials to engage individuals and raise awareness about the dangers of online radicalization.

Counter-Narrative Campaigns:

Counter-narrative initiatives aim to challenge extremist ideologies and provide alternative narratives that emphasize peace, tolerance, and the rejection of violence.

These campaigns often involve former extremists and survivors sharing their experiences to dissuade individuals from pursuing a path of violence.

Community Engagement:

Building strong, resilient communities is vital in preventing extremism. This involves community leaders, religious institutions, and grassroots organizations working together to foster tolerance, inclusivity, and social cohesion.

Community engagement initiatives often focus on developing mentorship programs, youth centers, and social activities that provide alternatives to extremist recruitment.

Law Enforcement and First Respondents Training:

Law enforcement agencies receive training on recognizing signs of radicalization and responding effectively to threats of violence. This training helps officers identify individuals in need of intervention while respecting civil liberties.

First respondents, such as paramedics and healthcare professionals, are also educated on recognizing potential indicators of radicalization and referring individuals for appropriate help.

Academic Research and Publications:

Academics and researchers contribute to the field of countering violent extremism by conducting studies and publishing research papers. This research helps policymakers and practitioners develop evidence-based strategies.

International Cooperation:

The global nature of extremism necessitates international cooperation. Nations often collaborate to share best practices, intelligence, and resources in the fight against violent extremism.

Evaluation and Adaptation:

Continuous assessment and evaluation of education and awareness programs are crucial to measure their effectiveness and make necessary adjustments.

Programs should be flexible and adaptable to address evolving threats and changing circumstances.

Education and awareness on violent extremism aim to reduce the appeal of extremist ideologies and prevent individuals from becoming radicalized. By promoting understanding, fostering resilience, and countering extremist narratives, these efforts contribute to a safer and more inclusive society.

CHAPTER SIX

Strengthening Family and Community Bonds

Strengthening family and community bonds plays a critical role in promoting social cohesion, resilience, and preventing various social issues, including violence, crime, substance abuse, and mental health problems. These bonds are essential for building strong, supportive, and inclusive societies. Here are accounts of the role of strengthening family and community bonds:

Social Support:

Strong family and community bonds provide individuals with a network of social support. This support is crucial during times of stress, crises, and personal challenges.

Families and communities that offer emotional, financial, and practical assistance can help individuals cope with difficulties and reduce the risk of them turning to harmful behaviors, such as substance abuse or violent extremism.

Child Development:

Healthy family relationships are vital for the cognitive, emotional, and social development of children. A stable and nurturing family environment contributes to positive child outcomes.

Communities that value and support families often provide resources, such as quality childcare, education, and extracurricular activities, which can enhance child development.

Crime Prevention:

Strong community bonds can serve as a crime prevention mechanism. When neighbors know and trust each other, they are more likely to watch out for one another and report suspicious activities to law enforcement.

Communities with close-knit relationships may implement neighborhood watch programs and other community policing initiatives, which can deter criminal activity.

Substance Abuse Prevention:

Families and communities that emphasize positive social norms, communication, and education about the dangers of substance abuse can significantly reduce the likelihood of individuals succumbing to addiction.

Strong community bonds can create environments where individuals find healthier, more fulfilling ways to socialize and cope with stress.

Mental Health Support:

Family and community bonds offer emotional and psychological support, which can be crucial in addressing mental health issues. Stigma surrounding mental health can be reduced in more supportive environments.

Communities may establish mental health awareness programs and support networks to help individuals access the help they need.

Social Cohesion:

Strong bonds among family members and community residents contribute to social cohesion, a sense of belonging, and shared identity. These factors foster cooperation, understanding, and mutual respect among individuals.

Socially cohesive communities are better equipped to address and prevent social issues, as members are more likely to work together to find solutions.

Resilience in Times of Crisis:

During natural disasters, economic downturns, or other crises, strong family and community bonds are essential for resilience. These bonds enable people to come together, share resources, and support one another.

Community organizations, such as local charities and relief agencies, often play a crucial role in coordinating disaster response efforts.

Inter-generational Transfer of Values:

Families serve as the primary means of passing down cultural, ethical, and moral values from one generation to the next. These values help shape the character and behaviors of individuals within a community.

Communities that value the preservation of these traditions and values tend to foster greater stability and social harmony.

Prevention of Radicalization:

Strengthening family bonds and community ties can help prevent individuals from becoming radicalized or engaging in violent extremism. When individuals feel a sense of belonging and support, they are less susceptible to extremist ideologies.

Long-Term Community Development:

Building and maintaining strong family and community bonds are integral to long-term community development. It fosters a sense of pride and investment in the local community, which can lead to economic growth, improved infrastructure, and overall well-being.

In summary, strengthening family and community bonds has far-reaching positive effects on individual and community well-being. These bonds provide emotional support, promote resilience, and play a significant role in preventing social issues and fostering a more inclusive and harmonious society.

CHAPTER SEVEN

Promoting Youth Engagement and Empowerment

Promoting youth engagement and empowerment is crucial for the personal development of young individuals and for the overall well-being of society. Empowering youth to actively participate in decision-making processes and contribute to their communities helps address various social issues, fosters civic responsibility, and ensures a brighter future. Here are details on promoting youth engagement and empowerment:

Civic Education:

Civic education programs are designed to inform young people about their rights, responsibilities, and the functioning of government and civil society.

These programs help young individuals understand the importance of participating in the democratic process, including voting and engaging in community activities.

Youth Leadership Development: Youth leadership development initiatives aim to identify and nurture young leaders. These programs provide training, mentorship, and opportunities for youth to take on leadership roles in their communities and organizations. Developing leadership skills empowers young people to become effective advocates for change and active contributors to their communities.

Youth Councils and Advisory Boards: Many communities and governments establish youth councils or advisory boards to ensure young people have a voice in decision-making processes. These councils allow youth to express their views, propose initiatives, and work with local authorities to address issues that affect them.

Volunteerism and Service Learning: Encouraging youth to engage in volunteerism and service learning activities not only empowers them to make a positive impact on their communities but also helps develop empathy and a sense of responsibility. These experiences allow young people to apply their skills and knowledge to real-world situations and gain a better understanding of societal challenges.

Access to Education and Training: Providing quality education and vocational training opportunities is essential for youth empowerment. Education equips young individuals with the knowledge and skills they need to succeed and contribute to society. Scholarships, grants, and subsidies can help ensure that all youth have access to education and training regardless of their socioeconomic background.

Entrepreneurship and Economic Empowerment: Initiatives that support entrepreneurship and economic empowerment for youth can help them become financially self-reliant and contribute to economic growth. Programs might include business training, access to microloans, and mentorship for young entrepreneurs.

Youth-Targeted Health and Well-being Programs: Promoting the physical and mental health of young people is critical. Programs that address issues like substance abuse, sexual health, and mental well-being empower youth to make informed choices and lead healthier lives. Access to healthcare and mental health support services is also crucial.

Online Engagement: Given the digital age, online platforms and social media play a significant role in engaging and empowering youth. Online spaces can be used for youth activism, advocacy, and information dissemination. Youth-led online campaigns can raise awareness and mobilize action on various social and political issues.

Encouraging Inclusivity and Diversity: Promoting diversity and inclusivity is essential for youth empowerment. Inclusive environments foster understanding and respect for various cultures, backgrounds, and perspectives. Creating safe spaces for dialogue and fostering intercultural exchanges can empower young people to bridge divides and build stronger communities.

Mentorship and Role Models: Mentoring programs connect young individuals with experienced mentors who can provide guidance, support, and encouragement. Positive role models and mentors can inspire youth, helping them navigate challenges and make informed decisions.

Youth Participation in Peace building: Empowering young people to participate in peace building efforts is crucial for conflict prevention and resolution. Youth can play a significant role in advocating for peaceful solutions to conflicts.

Youth-led peace initiatives can help reduce violence and promote dialogue in areas affected by conflict.

Promoting youth engagement and empowerment not only benefits young individuals but also strengthens communities and societies as a whole. Empowered youth are more likely to contribute positively to their communities, become responsible citizens, and lead fulfilling lives.

Countering Extremism Online

Countering Extremism Online" is a broad topic that encompasses various strategies and efforts to combat the spread of extremist ideologies and content on the internet. These efforts typically involve governments, tech companies, law enforcement agencies, non-governmental organizations, and researchers working together to prevent the dissemination of extremist propaganda and to counter the recruitment and radicalization of individuals online. Here are some key details and approaches related to countering extremism online:

Content Removal and Moderation: Many tech companies and social media platforms have policies in place to remove or restrict extremist content, hate speech, and related materials. They use automated algorithms and human moderators to identify and remove such content.

Hash Databases: Some organizations maintain databases of known extremist content in the form of digital "hashes." These databases can be used to identify and block or remove extremist content across multiple platforms.

Government Regulation: Some governments have introduced legislation and regulations to compel tech companies to take more proactive measures in countering extremism online. This has led to debates about the balance between free speech and online security.

Counter-Narrative Campaigns: Initiatives and organizations work to create and disseminate counter-narratives that challenge extremist ideologies. These campaigns aim to provide alternative viewpoints and narratives to those being targeted for radicalization.

Education and Awareness: Educational programs are developed to raise awareness about online extremism and the tactics used by extremist groups to recruit individuals. These programs target vulnerable populations, including young people.

Research and Analysis: Academics and researchers study online extremism to understand its causes and effects better. This research informs strategies for countering extremism online.

Collaborative Efforts: Many efforts involve international cooperation and information sharing to combat online extremism effectively. These include alliances, information sharing, and coordinated actions between governments and organizations.

Tech Tools: Some organizations and researchers have developed software tools and AI algorithms to identify and track online extremist activity and recruitment efforts.

De-radicalization Programs: Various initiatives work to rehabilitate individuals who have become involved with extremist ideologies and activities online. These programs focus on counseling, psychological support, and reintegration into society.

Ethical Dilemmas: Countering extremism online raises ethical questions about surveillance, privacy, and freedom of speech. Striking a balance between security and civil liberties is an ongoing challenge.

Efforts to counter extremism online continue to evolve, as extremist groups adapt to new technologies and platforms. It's important to find a balance between protecting individuals and societies from the harmful effects of online extremism while respecting fundamental principles of free expression and privacy.

Promoting Dialogue and Tolerance

"Promoting Dialogue and Tolerance" is a critical initiative aimed at fostering open and respectful communication among individuals and groups with diverse backgrounds, beliefs, and perspectives. The primary goal of this effort is to reduce prejudice, discrimination, and conflict while promoting understanding and acceptance. Here is an account of what promoting dialogue and tolerance entails:

1. Emphasis on Understanding: Promoting dialogue and tolerance encourages people to take the time to understand each other better, including their cultural, religious, and ideological differences. It starts with recognizing that diversity is a strength rather than a source of division.

2. Open Communication: Effective dialogue involves open and respectful communication where individuals are encouraged to express their thoughts and feelings without fear of judgment. This can take the form of face-to-face discussions, online forums, or community events.

3. Building Empathy: A key component of promoting tolerance is building empathy. This involves putting oneself in the shoes of others to better understand their experiences and perspectives. Empathy is a powerful tool for breaking down stereotypes and biases.

4. Education and Awareness: Promoting dialogue and tolerance often involves educational initiatives that raise awareness about the consequences of intolerance and discrimination. Schools, colleges, and community organizations play a crucial role in this regard.

5. Challenging Stereotypes: Encouraging people to question and challenge stereotypes and preconceived notions is essential for fostering tolerance. This involves dispelling myths and misconceptions about different groups of people.

6. Interfaith and Inter community Initiatives: Many efforts focus on bringing together individuals from different faiths and communities to engage in constructive dialogues, building bridges and common ground.

7. Conflict Resolution: Promoting dialogue and tolerance can also include training in conflict resolution techniques, which can be applied to interpersonal conflicts as well as larger social or international conflicts.

8. Cultural Exchange Programs: Programs that facilitate cultural exchanges and interactions among people fromdiverse backgrounds can be effective in promoting tolerance. These exchanges help break down barriers and foster understanding.

9. Celebrating Diversity: Embracing and celebrating the rich tapestry of diversity within society is a fundamental part of this initiative. Events and festivals that showcase various cultural traditions and perspectives can play a vital role in promoting tolerance.

10. Policy and Legislation: In some cases, governments enact policies and legislation to promote tolerance and reduce discrimination. These may include anti-discrimination laws, affirmative action programs, and other measures to ensure equal treatment and opportunities for all.

11. Grassroots Movements: Grassroots organizations, community leaders, and individuals often drive efforts to promote dialogue and tolerance. They play a critical role in creating inclusive and accepting communities.

Promoting dialogue and tolerance is a continuous process that requires the participation and commitment of individuals, communities, organizations, and governments. It is a vital response to the challenges of intolerance, discrimination, and prejudice in an increasingly diverse and interconnected world.

CHAPTER EIGHT

Digital Literacy and Online Safety

Digital literacy and online safety are essential skills and practices in the digital age. They encompass a range of knowledge and behaviors that enable individuals to use digital technologies safely, critically, and responsibly. Here are some key details regarding digital literacy and online safety:

Digital Literacy:

Definition: Digital literacy refers to the ability to access, understand, evaluate, and create content using digital technologies. It involves a combination of technical skills and critical thinking.

Skills and Competencies: Digital literacy encompasses a wide range of skills, including basic computer use, internet navigation, online research, data management, and proficiency in using software and applications.

Critical Thinking: Digital literacy includes the ability to critically assess the credibility and quality of online information and media. This is crucial to avoid misinformation and fake news.

Media Literacy: Understanding how media and digital content are created, distributed, and consumed is a key aspect of digital literacy. This includes recognizing bias, propaganda, and the influence of algorithms on content presentation.

Privacy Awareness: Digital literacy includes knowledge of online privacy and data security. Individuals should understand the importance of protecting their personal information and be able to adjust privacy settings on online platforms. Cybersecurity Awareness: Understanding common cybersecurity threats like phishing, malware, and online scams is essential. Knowing how to protect oneself from these threats is part of digital literacy.

Ethical Use: Digital literacy also involves understanding and practicing ethical behaviors online, including respecting copyright and intellectual property rights

.

Online Safety:

Definition: Online safety is the practice of protecting oneself and one's personal information while using the internet and digital technologies.

Password Management: Creating strong, unique passwords and using secure password management tools are crucial for online safety. It helps prevent unauthorized access to online accounts.

Two-Factor Authentication (2FA): Enabling 2FA adds an extra layer of security by requiring a second verification step, such as a code sent to a mobile device, when logging into an account.

Secure Browsing: Using secure and up-to-date web browsers, avoiding suspicious websites, and being cautious about clicking on unfamiliar links or downloading files are vital for online safety.

Social Media Awareness: Being mindful of the information shared on social media and adjusting privacy settings to control who can see one's posts and profile information is important.

Email Safety: Recognizing and avoiding phishing emails, which attempt to deceive individuals into revealing personal information, is a key aspect of online safety.

Safe Online Shopping: When making online purchases, individuals should use secure payment methods, shop from reputable websites, and be cautious about sharing financial information.

Digital Footprint Management: Understanding that online actions leave a digital footprint is essential. Being mindful of the information one shares and how it may impact their online and offline life is part of online safety.

Reporting and Blocking: Knowing how to report inappropriate content or behavior and how to block or mute users who engage in harassment or cyberbullying is crucial for maintaining online safety.

Children and Online Safety: Parents and caregivers play a role in teaching children about online safety, including age-appropriate content and online behavior guidelines.

Digital literacy and online safety go hand in hand, as individuals who are digitally literate are better equipped to protect themselves and navigate the online world safely. Both are ongoing processes, as technology evolves, and new digital challenges emerge. Education, awareness, and best practices are key components in promoting digital literacy and online safety.

Promoting dialogue and tolerance involves various strategies and initiatives aimed at fostering communication and understanding among diverse groups and individuals. Here are some brief details on this concept:

Interfaith and Interethnic Dialogues: These dialogues bring together people from different religious and ethnic backgrounds to engage in respectful discussions, share their perspectives, and build bridges of understanding. The goal is to reduce prejudice and promote religious and ethnic harmony.

Cultural Exchange Programs: These initiatives facilitate the exchange of culture, art, and ideas between different communities or nations. They help people appreciate the richness of different cultures and promote tolerance through shared experiences.

Education and Awareness: Promoting dialogue and tolerance often begins with education. Schools and organizations may implement programs that teach the value of tolerance, diversity, and respect for others, reducing discrimination and prejudice.

Conflict Resolution: Conflict resolution techniques and mediation play a vital role in promoting tolerance. These methods help address and resolve disputes in a non-violent and respectful manner, fostering understanding between conflicting parties.

Social Media and Digital Initiatives: Online platforms can be leveraged to promote dialogue and tolerance. Online campaigns, discussions, and social media movements can raise awareness and encourage conversations about tolerance and diversity.

Government Policies and Legislation: Some governments enact policies and laws that promote tolerance and diversity. These may include anti-discrimination laws, affirmative action, and initiatives to protect minority rights.

NGO and Civil Society Initiatives: Non-governmental organizations and civil society groups often take the lead in organizing events, workshops, and campaigns that encourage dialogue and tolerance. They work at the grassroots level to bring communities together.

Community Engagement: Building tolerance often starts at the community level. Encouraging residents to engage with one another, participate in community events, and interact with people from different backgrounds can help break down stereotypes and promote dialogue.

Media and Arts: The media, including film, television, literature, and art, can contribute to promoting tolerance by showcasing diverse perspectives and celebrating multiculturalism. Media plays a role in shaping public perceptions and attitudes.

Global Initiatives: International organizations and global initiatives, such as the United Nations' efforts to promote peace, tolerance, and understanding, work on a larger scale to address issues related to dialogue and tolerance on a global level.

Promoting dialogue and tolerance is essential for building harmonious and inclusive societies, reducing conflicts, and fostering peace and mutual respect among people of various backgrounds and beliefs.

CHAPTER NINE

Interfaith and Inter-ethnic Dialogue

Interfaith and interethnic dialogue can play a significant role in mitigating extremism by fostering understanding, promoting tolerance, and addressing the root causes of radicalization. Here's how these dialogues contribute to this effort:

Building Understanding and Trust: Interfaith and interethnic dialogues provide a platform for individuals from different religious and ethnic backgrounds to engage in open and respectful conversations. By doing so, they build mutual understanding and trust, which is essential in countering extremist narratives based on stereotypes and misconceptions.

Challenging Misconceptions: These dialogues allow participants to challenge and dispel misconceptions and prejudices they may have about other faiths or ethnic groups. This can help reduce the appeal of extremist ideologies that often rely on distorted or simplistic narratives about "the other."

Promoting Common Values: Interfaith and interethnic dialogues often emphasize shared values such as compassion, empathy, and peace. These shared values can serve as a counter-narrative to extremist ideologies that promote hatred, violence, and division.

Creating Alliances: By bringing together individuals and communities from diverse backgrounds, these dialogues help create alliances and networks of people who are committed to peaceful coexistence. These alliances can work together to counter the influence of extremist groups.

Preventing Radicalization: By providing a space for individuals to express their concerns and frustrations through dialogue rather than violence, these initiatives can help prevent the radicalization of disaffected individuals who might otherwise turn to extremism.

Resolving Conflicts: Interfaith and interethnic dialogues can address underlying conflicts and grievances that may be exploited by extremist groups. By offering a peaceful means of addressing grievances and disputes, these dialogues can reduce the appeal of extremist solutions.

Community Resilience: Communities engaged in interfaith and interethnic dialogues are often more resilient to extremist ideologies. They are better equipped to recognize and reject extremist propaganda and recruitment efforts within their midst.

Policy and Advocacy: The insights and relationships developed through these dialogues can inform policy and advocacy efforts aimed at countering extremism. Participants may work together to advocate for policies that promote diversity, tolerance, and social cohesion.

Crisis Response: In cases where extremist incidents occur, communities that have a history of interfaith and interethnic dialogue are often better equipped to respond effectively, maintain social cohesion, and prevent further radicalization.

While interfaith and interethnic dialogues are not a panacea for countering extremism, they are an important component of a broader strategy to prevent radicalization and promote peaceful coexistence. By addressing the underlying factors that contribute to extremism and by building bridges of understanding and cooperation, these dialogues contribute to a more resilient and inclusive society.

Dialogue is of paramount importance for several reasons, as it serves as a fundamental tool for communication, understanding, conflict resolution, and progress. Here are some key reasons highlighting the significance of dialogue:

Promotes Understanding: Dialogue allows individuals or groups with different perspectives, backgrounds, and experiences to exchange ideas and information. This, in turn, helps foster mutual understanding, empathy, and respect for one another.

Conflict Resolution: Dialogue is a peaceful and constructive means of resolving conflicts. It provides a platform for parties in dispute to express their concerns, negotiate, and find common ground, leading to peaceful resolutions without resorting to violence.

Fosters Cooperation: Dialogue is essential for building cooperation and collaboration. It enables people and organizations to work together towards common goals, whether in interpersonal relationships, business partnerships, or international diplomacy.

Facilitates Problem-Solving: Through open and honest conversations, dialogue helps identify and address problems or challenges effectively. It encourages creative thinking and the development of solutions to complex issues.

Encourages Inclusivity: Inclusive dialogue ensures that all voices and perspectives are heard, regardless of differences in gender, race, religion, or other characteristics. This inclusivity is vital for building diverse and equitable societies.

Enhances Learning: Engaging in dialogue is an opportunity to learn from others. By listening to different viewpoints and experiences, individuals can expand their knowledge and gain new insights, leading to personal and intellectual growth.

Strengthens Relationships: Dialogue is a cornerstone of healthy interpersonal relationships. It fosters trust, emotional connection, and intimacy, whether in personal, familial, or professional contexts.

Promotes Social Cohesion: In societies marked by diversity, dialogue is crucial for maintaining social cohesion. It helps bridge divides, reduce prejudice, and build a sense of shared identity and purpose among different groups.

Democratic Governance: In democratic societies, dialogue is central to the political process. It allows citizens to engage with their governments, express their opinions, and participate in decision-making, ensuring accountable and representative governance.

Cultural Exchange: Dialogue enables the exchange of culture, art, and ideas between different communities, fostering multiculturalism and global understanding. It helps preserve and celebrate cultural diversity.

Prevents Misunderstandings: Effective dialogue can prevent misunderstandings, miscommunication, and misinterpretation of intentions, reducing the potential for conflicts and disputes.

Promotes Peace and Tolerance: Dialogue is a key tool for promoting peace and tolerance on both a local and global scale. It can help address the underlying causes of conflict, counter extremism, and build bridges among communities.

In summary, dialogue is a foundational element of human interaction and societal progress. It facilitates understanding, cooperation, and the peaceful resolution of conflicts, making it a cornerstone of harmonious relationships, peaceful coexistence, and societal development.

The importance of dialogue

Dialogue is of paramount importance for several reasons, as it serves as a fundamental tool for communication, understanding, conflict resolution, and progress. Here are some key reasons highlighting the significance of dialogue:

Promotes Understanding: Dialogue allows individuals or groups with different perspectives, backgrounds, and experiences to exchange ideas and information. This, in turn, helps foster mutual understanding, empathy, and respect for one another.

Conflict Resolution: Dialogue is a peaceful and constructive means of resolving conflicts. It provides a platform for parties in dispute to express their concerns, negotiate, and find common ground, leading to peaceful resolutions without resorting to violence.

Fosters Cooperation: Dialogue is essential for building cooperation and collaboration. It enables people and organizations to work together towards common goals, whether in interpersonal relationships, business partnerships, or international diplomacy.

Facilitates Problem-Solving: Through open and honest conversations, dialogue helps identify and address problems or challenges effectively. It encourages creative thinking and the development of solutions to complex issues.

Encourages Inclusivity: Inclusive dialogue ensures that all voices and perspectives are heard, regardless of differences in gender, race, religion, or other characteristics. This inclusivity is vital for building diverse and equitable societies.

Enhances Learning: Engaging in dialogue is an opportunity to learn from others. By listening to different viewpoints and experiences, individuals can expand their knowledge and gain new insights, leading to personal and intellectual growth.

Strengthens Relationships: Dialogue is a cornerstone of healthy interpersonal relationships. It fosters trust, emotional connection, and intimacy, whether in personal, familial, or professional contexts.

Promotes Social Cohesion: In societies marked by diversity, dialogue is crucial for maintaining social cohesion. It helps bridge divides, reduce prejudice, and build a sense of shared identity and purpose among different groups.

Democratic Governance: In democratic societies, dialogue is central to the political process. It allows citizens to engage with their governments, express their opinions, and participate in decision-making, ensuring accountable and representative governance.

Cultural Exchange: Dialogue enables the exchange of culture, art, and ideas between different communities, fostering multiculturalism and global understanding. It helps preserve and celebrate cultural diversity.

Prevents Misunderstandings: Effective dialogue can prevent misunderstandings, miscommunication, and misinterpretation of intentions, reducing the potential for conflicts and disputes.

Promotes Peace and Tolerance: Dialogue is a key tool for promoting peace and tolerance on both a local and global scale. It can help address the underlying causes of conflict, counter extremism, and build bridges among communities.

In summary, dialogue is a foundational element of human interaction and societal progress. It facilitates understanding, cooperation, and the peaceful resolution of conflicts, making it a cornerstone of harmonious relationships, peaceful coexistence, and societal development.

Building bridges between communities is essential for promoting understanding, cooperation, and social cohesion in diverse societies. Here are some strategies and principles for effectively building bridges between different communities:

Open and Respectful Communication: Establish open channels of communication that allow communities to engage in respectful and honest dialogue. Encourage active listening, empathy, and the free exchange of ideas.

Foster Inclusivity: Ensure that all communities have a seat at the table and that their voices are heard and respected. Inclusivity promotes a sense of belonging and equality.

Cultural Exchange and Education: Organize cultural exchange programs, educational workshops, and events that help communities learn about each other's traditions, history, and values. This can dispel stereotypes and foster appreciation for diversity.

Collaborative Projects: Encourage communities to collaborate on projects or initiatives that address common concerns or benefit the broader society. Joint efforts can build trust and a sense of shared purpose.

Interfaith and Interethnic Dialogue: Promote dialogues and discussions that bring different religious and ethnic groups together. These dialogues can facilitate understanding, tolerance, and conflict resolution.

Community Events: Host events, festivals, and gatherings that celebrate the cultures, traditions, and contributions of different communities. These events provide opportunities for social interaction and foster a sense of unity.

Community Leadership: Encourage leaders from various communities to work together in addressing common issues. These leaders can serve as role models for cooperation and collaboration.

Promote Diversity in Institutions: Encourage diversity and inclusion in educational institutions, workplaces, and government bodies. Representation matters, and diverse decision-making bodies can better address the needs of all communities.

Address Discrimination and Prejudice: Work to eliminate discrimination and prejudice at systemic and individual levels. Implement policies and practices that promote fairness and equal treatment for all.

Peace and Reconciliation Initiatives: In regions with a history of conflict or division, support peace and reconciliation initiatives that bring communities together to heal wounds and build trust.

Media and Public Awareness: Encourage the media to portray diverse communities accurately and positively. Raise public awareness about the benefits of diversity and the importance of building bridges.

Conflict Resolution Training: Provide training in conflict resolution and mediation to community leaders and members, enabling them to address disputes peacefully and constructively.

Local Governance and Decision-Making: Empower local communities to have a say in governance and decision-making processes that affect them. This can promote a sense of ownership and cooperation.

Youth Engagement: Engage young people from different communities in joint activities, educational programs, and leadership opportunities. Young people are often open to building bridges and can be powerful agents of change.

Long-Term Commitment: Building bridges is a long-term process that requires ongoing commitment. Foster relationships and collaborations that endure over time.

Building bridges between communities is essential for creating more inclusive, tolerant, and harmonious societies. It requires proactive efforts, patience, and a commitment to promoting diversity and understanding as strengths rather than sources of division.

CHAPTER TEN

Fostering Empathy and Understanding

Fostering empathy and understanding plays a crucial role in addressing and preventing violent extremism by addressing underlying issues and promoting positive social change. Here are several ways in which this approach can contribute to curbing violent extremism:

Countering Dehumanization: Violent extremism often relies on dehumanizing "the other" to justify acts of violence. Fostering empathy encourages individuals to see the humanity in others, making it more challenging for extremist ideologies to take root.

Building Bridges: Empathy helps build bridges between diverse communities, fostering a sense of unity and shared humanity. When people from different backgrounds understand and appreciate each other, the likelihood of radicalization decreases.

Addressing Root Causes: Empathy encourages a deeper understanding of the root causes of extremism, such as socioeconomic disparities, political instability, and cultural tensions. By addressing these underlying issues, it becomes possible to create more sustainable solutions.

Promoting Inclusivity: Emphasizing empathy promotes inclusivity and tolerance, reducing the appeal of extremist ideologies that thrive on exclusion and division. Inclusive societies are less likely to foster the grievances that extremists exploit.

Encouraging Dialogue: Open and honest dialogue is essential for breaking down barriers and dispelling misunderstandings. Fostering empathy creates a conducive environment for constructive conversations that challenge extremist narratives.

Preventing Radicalization: Empathy education can act as a preventive measure by teaching critical thinking skills and resilience against extremist propaganda. Individuals who are empathetic are more likely to question radical ideas and resist recruitment efforts.

Supporting Rehabilitation: For individuals who have already been radicalized, empathy is a key component of rehabilitation. Programs that focus on empathy and understanding can help reintegrate former extremists into society, addressing the root causes of their radicalization.

Promoting Education: Educational initiatives centered around empathy and understanding contribute to creating informed and enlightened societies. Knowledgeable individuals are less susceptible to manipulation by extremist ideologies.

Media Literacy: Fostering empathy includes teaching individuals to critically analyze media messages. Media literacy helps people recognize and reject extremist propaganda, reducing its impact.

Building Resilient Communities: Empathetic communities are more resilient to the divisive tactics employed by extremists. When people feel connected to their communities, they are less likely to be swayed by extremist ideologies that seek to undermine social cohesion.

It's important to note that fostering empathy and understanding is just one part of a comprehensive strategy to address violent extremism. It should be complemented by efforts to address structural inequalities, promote good governance, and provide opportunities for positive social and economic development. Additionally, collaboration between governments, civil society, and communities is essential for the success of such initiatives.

Real-World Success Stories - Profiles of individuals who turned away from extremism - Communities that have successfully countered extremism

While specific profiles of individuals who turned away from extremism may not always be readily available due to privacy and security concerns, there are stories of people who have disengaged from extremist ideologies and found paths to rehabilitation. Additionally, there are examples of communities and initiatives that have successfully countered extremism. Here are a few general examples:

Christian Picciolini (United States): Christian Picciolini is a former white supremacist who co-founded the organization Life After Hate. After leaving the extremist movement, he dedicated his life to helping others disengage from hate groups. Life After Hate provides support and resources for individuals seeking to leave extremist ideologies behind.

Mubin Shaikh (Canada): Mubin Shaikh was involved in extremist activities in his youth but later renounced his involvement. He became an informant for Canadian intelligence and has since worked as a counter-terrorism expert, advocating for dialogue and understanding between communities.

Maajid Nawaz (United Kingdom): Maajid Nawaz was a former member of the Islamist group Hizb ut-Tahrir. After his release from prison in Egypt, he underwent a transformation and co-founded the Quilliam Foundation, an organization dedicated to countering extremism. Nawaz now advocates for a more tolerant and inclusive understanding of Islam.

Hoda Muthana (United States): Hoda Muthana left the United States to join ISIS but later expressed regret and a desire to return home. While her case is controversial, it highlights the complexities of individuals disengaging from extremist groups and the challenges they may face upon returning.

De-Radicalization Initiatives in Indonesia: Indonesia has implemented various successful de-radicalization programs, including efforts to reintegrate former extremists into society. The country's approach combines religious counseling, vocational training, and community engagement to address the root causes of radicalization.

Strong Cities Network Initiatives: Various cities within the Strong Cities Network have implemented successful community-based initiatives to counter extremism. For example, the city of Aarhus in Denmark, as mentioned earlier, has been recognized for its early intervention model, which includes community engagement, education, and social services.

The "Extreme Dialogue" Project (Canada, UK, Germany): The Extreme Dialogue project features stories of individuals who have disengaged from extremism, providing a platform for them to share their experiences. The project aims to challenge extremist narratives and promote understanding through multimedia resources.

These examples illustrate the importance of tailored interventions, community involvement, and rehabilitation efforts in countering extremism. Successful stories often involve a combination of factors, including mentorship, education, community support, and opportunities for individuals to reintegrate into society.

Moving Forward - The way ahead - The role of every Nigerian youth

Moving forward, the role of every Nigerian youth is crucial in shaping the future of the country. Here are several key aspects where Nigerian youth can make a positive impact:

Education and Skill Development:

Advocate for Quality Education: Nigerian youth can advocate for policies that prioritize and enhance the quality of education in the country.

Continuous Learning: Embrace opportunities for skill development and continuous learning, which are essential for personal and professional growth.

Entrepreneurship and Economic Development:

Promote Entrepreneurship: Engage in entrepreneurial activities to contribute to economic growth and job creation.

Support Local Businesses: Prioritize supporting local businesses and startups to strengthen the national cconomy.

Social and Political Engagement:

Participate in Civic Activities: Get involved in civic activities, such as voting, community development projects, and volunteering, to contribute to positive social change.

Advocate for Good Governance: Advocate for transparency, accountability, and good governance at both local and national levels.

Technology and Innovation:

Embrace Technology: Utilize technology for personal and professional development, and explore innovative solutions to address societal challenges.

Promote STEM Education: Advocate for the promotion of Science,Ttechnology, Engineering, and Mathematics (STEM) education to prepare for a tech-driven future.

Environmental Conservation:

Sustainable Practices: Embrace sustainable practices in daily life and advocate for environmental conservation to address issues such as climate change and deforestation.

Health and Well-being:

Promote Health Awareness: Advocate for health awareness and engage in activities that promote physical and mental well-being.

Support Healthcare Initiatives: Support healthcare initiatives and programs that address public health challenges.

Social Harmony and Inclusivity:

Foster Inclusivity: Promote inclusivity, tolerance, and unity among diverse communities to build a more harmonious society.

Combat Extremism: Actively work towards countering extremism by promoting dialogue, understanding, and cooperation.

Media Literacy:

Promote Critical Thinking: Advocate for media literacy and critical thinking to combat the spread of misinformation and fake news.

Utilize Social Media Responsibly: Use social media responsibly and ethically, contributing positively to public discourse.

Women's Empowerment:

Support Gender Equality: Advocate for gender equality and support initiatives that empower women and girls in education, employment, and leadership roles.

Global Collaboration:

Engage in Diplomacy: Support diplomatic efforts and engage in international collaboration to address global challenges and foster positive relations with other nations.

The future of Nigeria lies in the hands of its youth. By actively participating in various aspects of society, Nigerian youth can contribute to positive change, economic development, and the overall well-being of the nation. Building a prosperous and harmonious future requires a collective effort, and the energy, creativity, and passion of the youth are invaluable assets in this endeavor.

IN SUMMARY,

Preventing violent extremism among Nigerian youths involves a multifaceted approach that addresses the root causes and employs various strategies.

1. **Education and Awareness:**
   - Promote education as a tool for empowerment, critical thinking, and tolerance.
   - Develop and implement awareness campaigns to educate youths about the dangers of violent extremism, its consequences, and alternative paths.
2. **Youth Empowerment:**
   - Create opportunities for skill development,

vocational training, and employment to empower youths economically.
  - o Support entrepreneurship initiatives to encourage self-reliance and financial stability.
3. **Community Engagement:**
  - o Strengthen community bonds to create a sense of belonging and purpose.
  - o Encourage open dialogue within communities to address grievances and concerns.
4. **Religious and Cultural Tolerance:**
  - o Promote interfaith dialogue and understanding to foster religious tolerance.
  - o Emphasize the diversity of cultures in Nigeria, encouraging acceptance and appreciation for different traditions.
5. **Media Literacy:**
  - o Develop programs that enhance media literacy to help youths critically analyze and interpret information.
  - o Counter extremist narratives through positive and inclusive messaging.
6. **Counseling and Rehabilitation:**
  - o Establish counseling services for individuals who may be susceptible to radicalization.
  - o Implement rehabilitation programs for those who have already been involved in extremist activities.
7. **Government Policies and Support:**
  - o Advocate for policies that address socio-economic disparities and provide support for marginalized communities.
  - o Ensure inclusive governance that addresses the needs and concerns of all segments of the population.
8. **International Collaboration:**

- Collaborate with international organizations and neighboring countries to share best practices and intelligence.
- Engage in cross-border initiatives to address the transnational nature of extremist activities.

9. **Youth Involvement in Decision-Making:**
   - Encourage the active participation of youths in decision-making processes at local and national levels.
   - Provide platforms for youths to express their concerns and contribute to policy development.

10. **Monitoring Online Activities:**
    - Increase efforts to monitor and counter online radicalization.
    - Collaborate with tech companies to identify and remove extremist content from online platforms.

11. **Early Warning Systems:**
    - Develop and implement early warning systems to identify potential radicalization indicators.
    - Train community leaders, educators, and law enforcement to recognize signs of extremism.

12. **Legal Framework:**
    - Strengthen legal frameworks to prosecute those involved in recruiting or engaging in violent extremist activities.
    - Ensure that the legal system is fair, transparent, and respects human rights.

By addressing these aspects comprehensively, Nigeria can work towards creating an environment that is less conducive to violent extremism among its youth population. It requires a collaborative effort from the government, civil society, communities, and international partners.

References:

1. **Studies in Conflict & Terrorism**
   - Publisher: Taylor & Francis
   - Website: Studies in Conflict & Terrorism
2. **Terrorism and Political Violence**
   - Publisher: Taylor & Francis
   - Website: Terrorism and Political Violence
3. **Perspectives on Terrorism**
   - Publisher: Terrorism Research Initiative
   - Website: Perspectives on Terrorism
4. **Journal of Terrorism Research**
   - Publisher: University of St Andrews
   - Website: Journal of Terrorism Research
5. **Security Dialogue**
   - Publisher: SAGE Journals
   - Website: Security Dialogue
6. **Critical Studies on Terrorism**
   - Publisher: Taylor & Francis
   - Website: Critical Studies on Terrorism
7. **Studies in Conflict & Terrorism**
   - Publisher: Taylor & Francis
   - Website: Studies in Conflict & Terrorism
8. **Global Crime**
   - Publisher: Taylor & Francis
   - Website: Global Crime
9. **Journal of Strategic Security**
   - Publisher: Henley-Putnam School of Strategic Security
   - Website: Journal of Strategic Security
10. **International Journal of Conflict and Violence**
    - Publisher: PsychOpen
11. Website: International Journal of Conflict and Violence
Akinbi, J.O (2015). "Examining the Boko Haram

Insurgency in Northern Nigeria and the Quest for a
Permanent Resolution of the Crisis". Global Journal of Arts,
Humanities and Social Sciences Vol.3, №8, pp.32–45.
12. Awojobi, O.N (2014). "The Socio-Economic Implications
of Boko Haram Insurgency in the North-East of Nigeria".
International Journal of Innovation and Scientific Research.
Vol. 11 №1. pp. 144–150.

Glossary of Terms

1. **Violent Extremism:**
   o Violent extremism refers to the advocacy, support,
     or use of violence to achieve ideological, religious,
     or political goals. It often involves radicalization,
     where individuals or groups adopt extreme beliefs
     and resort to violent means to achieve their
     objectives.
2. **Radicalization:**
   o Radicalization is the process by which an individual
     or group adopts extreme beliefs, ideologies, or
     political views. It can lead to the endorsement or
     use of violence as a means to achieve those beliefs.
3. **Terrorism:**
   o Terrorism involves the use of violence or
     intimidation, typically targeting civilians, to create
     fear and advance political, ideological, or religious
     objectives. It often aims to instigate political change
     or draw attention to a particular cause.
4. **Counterterrorism (CT):**
   o Counterterrorism refers to measures taken by
     governments, security forces, and communities to
     prevent, respond to, and mitigate the impact of

terrorist activities. It includes intelligence, law enforcement, and military efforts.

5. **Countering Violent Extremism (CVE):**
    - CVE encompasses a broader set of strategies aimed at preventing the radicalization and recruitment of individuals into violent extremist groups. It includes initiatives focused on addressing underlying social, economic, and political factors.
6. **Deradicalization:**
    - Deradicalization involves the process of disengaging individuals or groups from radical ideologies and violent extremist activities. It often includes psychological counseling, education, and rehabilitation programs.
7. **Jihad:**
    - Jihad is an Arabic term that translates to "struggle" or "striving." In Islam, it can refer to the personal struggle for spiritual growth, but it has also been interpreted in various ways, including armed struggle or holy war.
8. **Salafism:**
    - Salafism is a conservative Sunni Islamic movement that advocates a return to the perceived practices of the "salaf," the early generations of Muslims. While not inherently violent, some Salafist groups have been associated with extremist ideologies.
9. **Propaganda:**
    - Propaganda refers to information, often biased or misleading, disseminated to promote a particular viewpoint or agenda. In the context of violent extremism, propaganda can be used to recruit and radicalize individuals.
10. **Foreign Fighters:**
    - Foreign fighters are individuals who travel to a

foreign country to participate in armed conflicts, often aligned with extremist groups. The term gained prominence in the context of individuals joining conflicts such as those in Syria and Iraq.

11. **Insurgency:**
   o   Insurgency involves armed rebellion against an established authority or government. Insurgent groups may employ guerrilla warfare tactics to challenge the existing political order.

These definitions provide a foundational understanding of key terms related to violent extremism, but the nuances and interpretations of these terms can vary in different contexts.

ABOUT THE AUTHOR

I, Onuche E. Samson, considers this platform a privilege to be involved, haven participated, encouraged and inspired a lot of Young Minds in the Society through my Youth Engaging Platform: "The Kogi Earnest Group-KEG", participated in the "Not Too Young To Run"-pre-2015, Actively participated in the YALI Network in Collaboration with the US Embassy-Accountability and Transparency Summit of 2018, Abuja.

I was the 3rd Runner Up in the Country, in the Action Aid Nigeria, Essay Competition on the Role of Youths in the fight against "Violent Extremism".

As the Coordinator of the Kogi Earnest Group-KEG, I, alongside with my Co-founder, ensures the youths are actively involved in building their communities, ensuring, safety and clean environment, also, encouraging them to actively participate in the electoral decisions of their host communities and be the change agents of the new Nigeria, we all clamour to see. It is a project of a lifetime, which we are still engaged in doing to serve as the voice of the youths across, the 21 local government areas of Kogi State and cutting across both political and non political divides. In a bid to foster Unity of purpose, the KEG members and management teams are drawn from each of the local governments producing at least 3 nominees, as part of the national organizing team and one person each from the various wards in the state. We are also, expanding it to become a pan Nigerian platform. Late 2018, the group distributed about a 100 copies of Novels on the topic "Entwined" to 20 secondary schools in Lokoja Metropolis in attendance was the former GTBANK Lokoja Branch Manager, Ibrahim Odoma.

As a Young Graduate of 2015, I Co-authored an Academic Journal on the "Location-Allocation of Worship Centers, with 5 other Federal University of Technology, Minna Lecturers, this journal seeks to address the issue of community noise pollution emanating from the worship centers around our residential areas, a case study of Mina Metropolis with a designed model and a constrain introduced to give us a bench mark on the limit and effects of such noise around the neighborhood within a specified period.

I am a father and a husband to my lovely wife Mrs Dorcas Amodu-Onuche with my lovely Kid, Deborah Uraojo Eunice (DUE).

I am passionate about seeing a working Nigeria, a country that all of us can be proud of, it begins with you and I taking the right decision at the right time, not waiting until things go wrong before trying to address it, being proactive is my watch ward. As Election Day draws near, I encourage everyone of us to go all out and make the right choice of whom should be our leader regardless of where such person is coming from, regardless of his religious or ethnic backgrounds, we must think as Nigerian than as an individual.

I am currently, the Deputy Director/Board Secretary of a Partnership between RWEYDF and Federal University Lokoja ICT Training Institute, Lokoja, with board members such as Professor MS Audu, DVC Academy, The Newly Appointed VC of Thomas Adewumi University, Oke, Kwara State, who was the Director and former HOD, Computer Department of FUL Lokoja, before her appointment as the VC.

I am an Entrepreneur with interest in the Agro and ICT, currently nursing an EleDan Farm, an affiliate of the De-Galaxy EleDan Services Nig. Ltd.

An awardee of:

(a) Global Community Engagement and Resilience Fund (GCERF)

b) The GYBCEDO EbIgO Entrepreneurship Scheme (NGO)

Thank you

www.ingramcontent.com/pod-product-compliance
Lightning Source LLC
Chambersburg PA
CBHW071054260726
48661CB00006B/2270